Cryptocurrency

The Complete Manual For New Investors To Invest In
The Crypto Market And Trade Bitcoins

(A Manual For Constructing Mining Rigs And Mining Bitcoin)

Alphonse Ramos

TABLE OF CONTENT

Introduction And Divergence Rules 1
Development Of Cryptocurrencies 30
What Is Cryptocurrency? 47
Cryptocurrency And Blockchain 70
Starting With Bitcoin 84
Basics Of Cryptocurrency 113
Why Do Cryptocurrencies Exist? 143

Introduction And Divergence Rules

One of the most popular indicators used to help investors make choices is divergence. Divergence may help you determine the general direction a trend is going when you can recognize it clearly. In this way, you may predict the likely trend reversal to a considerable degree.

It's crucial to keep in mind that you may benefit from either a bullish or bearish trend when employing divergence to establish your trading strategy. Everything relies on how quickly you can identify the trend's potential for reversal.

Because of this, the emphasis of this chapter is on leveraging divergence as a tactic to swiftly and efficiently set up your transactions. The essential thing to remember is that you must recognize the divergence in order to benefit from it.

The relationship between trend and moving average is what most trading manuals state determines divergence. Moving average convergence divergence, or MACD, is the name given to this method.

When using the MACD approach, you are simply looking for the places when the moving average and trendline will cross. Although this method is quite useful, it might result in misleading signals since the moving average is just one indicator you can use to determine the overall trend pattern of the currency pair you are monitoring.

In order to provide you a clear and precise picture of when reversals are likely to occur, we will utilize Price Action as a method of assessing divergence in this chapter. You'll discover that this method works best for identifying divergence so you can set up entry and exit points. The best part is that you are just utilizing pricing, which is the most accurate indication, as your only indicator.

There are several useful pointers to bear in mind while using divergence as a strategy:

- Ensure that the highs and lows are higher than the previous high and lower than the previous low, respectively. This implies that in order to detect divergence, your highs and lows must both break out. You'll be able to receive the proper tracking for the desired divergence when you locate there. The simplest method to recognize this is by looking for double tops and bottoms.

• The tops and bottoms must be arranged in ascending order. You must thus look out for sudden dips and surges. Smaller dips and spikes won't work; all you could be seeing is an increase in trade volume.

• Check that the trendline is headed in the appropriate direction to connect the tops or bottoms you are interested in. If not, you risk entering too early or too late. This is significant because the trendline's intersection with a major top or major bottom marks the location of the reversal.

Additionally, please make sure to consider various periods. You won't get the whole image if you simply pay attention to the tone period. Please keep in mind that anything might happen quickly. Therefore, it's always advisable to travel farther back in time to support your plan. You may then be quite certain that you are headed in the correct direction.

Strategies for Entry and Exit Using Divergence

When determining entry and exit positions as part of your overall trading strategy, divergence is a very beneficial tool. Divergence primarily serves as a signal for when to enter and when to exit a situation. It should be remembered that during a bearish trend, the ideal entry position is at the lowest point. The highest point during a bullish trend, however, would be the perfect time to exit. In any of these scenarios, it would be desirable to enter or exit just before the shift in trend occurs. This will enable you to increase your earnings in any case. So let's look at how you might profit from this circumstance.

Let's begin with a negative trend first.

A negative trend by definition denotes a downward tendency in the price movement as a whole. Even if there are notable peaks along the way, you may still ascertain that your trendline is downward sloping. You need to predict when the trend will change when this happens.

Finding the best place to enter a trade setup is the primary goal of playing a bearish trend. when a result, you are searching for the lowest point just when the trend is about to change. The intersection of the trendline with the lowest point of the price movement is theoretically at this location. However, this point must be at least as low as the support level allows.

Consequently, determining the support level is the first step in making this method effective. A double bottom would be an excellent sign that this strategy would be successful. You may attempt to focus just on one success. That doesn't guarantee that the pattern will change, however. It would be a false signal if it happened. Therefore, the best sign is a double bottom. If a triple bottom is seen without the trendline crossing, prepare for a significant takeoff.

When you locate the precise position where the trendline and the support level connect, you will know where to enter the market. You may start trading from here. The price will then likely skyrocket. Your risk to reward ratio determines where to turn around. Your exit may be positioned anywhere between 20 and 60 pip above your entrance. It would be advised, nonetheless, that you confirm prior highs. The greatest indicator of where you can predict the peak will occur will come from this.

Let's now examine this bullish trend-based trading method.

Finding the optimal escape is the whole goal of this method. The goal of this exit strategy is to increase your revenue. As a result, the goal is to exit the trade at its maximum position just before the trend changes.

It's crucial to determine the resistance level in order to achieve this. You should ideally have a double top that you may use as a guide. You could be seeing a misleading signal if your double top has a point that has broken out of the resistance level band. The increasing trade volume is often to blame for this. You must maintain the double top at or very near the resistance level for this arrangement to function properly. If there isn't a breakthrough after a triple top, the downturn will be severe. Therefore, positioning your exit point a little bit before the resistance level limit can be a smart idea.

Automatically setting up stop-loss and take-profit points is crucial in both situations since it will prevent you from falling asleep at the wheel. If you won't be physically present at your terminal, this is very crucial. In these circumstances, when your particular point is triggered, the market orders will immediately be activated. Please remember that automating your take-profit and stop-loss points will save you a ton of problems in the future.

Divergence Drawdown Management

Drawdown is one of the major problems FOREX traders have while using the divergence technique. Drawdown happens when many stops are hit at different times during a trading cycle. The price may automatically drop when a large number of stops are abruptly struck, leaving investors with no profit. In fact, a quick drop might result in more pauses.

This explains why unexpected price drops are so frequent. It's not so much that there has been a rapid change in investor sentiment; rather, the market responds when many stops are activated simultaneously. It might be challenging to turn a profit as the price declines and more stops are activated.

Sadly, some investors discover that their investments are sold before they reach the take-profit level. This is all a result of stops being triggered automatically.

Investors sometimes choose not to set up automatic stop-loss settings in order to avoid being liquidated during a decline, which is a typical error. To put it mildly, this is a risky circumstance. You are definitely playing with fire. It's possible that the activity heats up and intensifies quite quickly. You may not have enough time to respond as a result. You cannot thus expect your human reactions to respond more quickly than a machine.

Divergence trading is not a precise science, which is another crucial point to remember. You must be aware that it is by no means a flawless technique since stops might suddenly be activated all at once. Because of this, structuring your offer properly can assist you avoid being eliminated from the competition before you have the opportunity to make a profit.

It should be highlighted that you must make sure to control your inclinations. You may not have a chance to go that high if you chose to set up your take-profit points too high. As a consequence, unexpected drawdowns will knock you out.

One last thing to be aware of is that your stop-loss point will be significantly lower if you enter at the bottom of the trend than it would be for an investor who entered later. As a consequence, keeping an appropriate risk to reward ratio will make it much simpler for you to handle drawdowns.

Think about this scenario:

You correctly predicted the trend's bottom and its impending reversal. As a result, you are now in position 1. You made the choice to place your stop at 20 pip. With a risk to reward ratio of 2:1, this would place your stop-loss at 0.80. As a result, you decide that 1.40 will be your take-profit level (20 pip * 2; this is the 2:1 ratio).

If the price reaches 1.41 with this strategy, your trade will be closed off as soon as you reach your automatic take-profit level. This denotes a lucrative transaction. The world is wonderful, and you earn money. Let's presume, though, that you are experiencing b0ld. You decide on a risk to reward ratio of 3:1. Your take-profit point now stands at 1.60. However, since they enter the market later, investors place their stops at around 1.45. Prices drop below 1.45 after a sharp decline at around 1.47. A number of stops are automatically initiated by this. The price does not rise over 1.40 due to the liquidation of many positions. However, you are constrained to a 1.60 take-profit point.

Do you see why, if you set your take-profit point too high, you may never reach it?

Because of this, astute traders are aware that it's ideal to put up transactions that are grounded in reality. You could be better off placing your take profit point below this range, for example, if the price of the currency pairing seems to be trending at a maximum of 1.50. By doing this, you can make sure that you don't make your expectations too high and end up disappointed.

Keeping Divergence Drawdown at Bay

Examining the resistance level for the currency pair you are watching is the simplest technique to prevent divergence decline. Even while you may be tempted to place your take-profit point just at the peak of the wave, you should probably reconsider. A reversal might be imminent if you see a double top. It could be preferable in this situation to position your escape point just under that threshold. Five pip differences may be significant.

Being prepared to avert drawdown is a crucial additional strategy. When there is a lot of trade, you can know a downturn is imminent. You could be interested in keeping an eye out if you see that several deals are taking place at once. Sell right away if you observe that the price has stabilized. The more quickly you can close out your position, the more money you'll earn. This is crucial since it will allow you to generate a profit that is acceptable rather than having it wiped out by an unexpected influx of stops. Depending on how quickly you can respond, this is often a useful technique to save your earnings from being completely lost.

Finally, playing it cautious is an excellent strategy for avoiding drawdowns. If you close out your position well in advance of the trend's reversal, you may think about re-entering the play later on, but this time with a much tighter position—perhaps one with a 1:1 risk to reward ratio—just to be careful.

Finding the Correct Divergence Setups

Divergence configurations may be difficult to recognize. We have now covered the key elements required to accurately identify a probable divergence configuration. Therefore, it's crucial to discuss any potential misleading signals that you can run across while looking into a setup.

A trendline that does not seem to connect the resistance or support level is the first misleading indication to be aware of. Therefore, even if there is no trendline to cross, you may have two or even three peaks and bottoms. When searching for an entry point, for example, you could be inclined to believe that things might reverse. However, you could discover that under these circumstances, a breakthrough is considerably more likely.

A trendline that is swaying sideways is another erroneous warning to be on the lookout for. Entering into this discussion is quite risky. If you are careless, you can wind yourself into a deal in which you will lose out. Always watch for the candlesticks when there is a sideways trendline. Be prepared to leave if you see that the candlesticks are pointing downward. In this scenario, setting up at a very tight stop and profit point, such as 10 pip each way, is an option. In a situation like this, your goal is to make a rapid profit and get out of there.

The absence of a distinct trend is yet another misleading indicator. Although there may be two or three tops and bottoms, there is no clearly defined trendline. The trendline in this instance may resemble a wave or may have really acute spikes and dips. The outcome of increasing trade activity may be this. It may simply suggest that stock investors, for instance, are switching to FOREX as a strategy to temporarily avoid equities. Therefore, please attempt to steer clear of utilizing the tops and bottoms alone to guide your setup. The trendline has to be watched carefully. Otherwise, a misleading signal might lead you to enter a transaction. Although there's a chance you'll get fortunate, there's also a good chance you'll fail.

Confluence and Divergence

When two or more indicators cross paths on a chart, confluence occurs. As a result, you must consider a number of signs to make sure that your configuration is appropriate. The MACD is the most used tool for doing this kind of research.

You must employ the moving average of the currency pair you are trading in this kind of technique. The MACD will let you see both the price activity and the moving average of the price in question in this respect. Confluence occurs when both of these indications are traveling in unison toward a junction. Divergence occurs when they are veering apart from one another. You may utilize one of these situations to determine where you should make your next move.

Confluence will be discussed first.

When a price action trendline and moving average are growing closer to one another, confluence occurs. If a moving average is bullish and there is a bearish trendline, then the trend may be about to reverse. The intersection of the two lines is where the reversal happens. They should meet someplace at or close to the support level, where they should intersect. The lines will start to diverge after they have crossed one another. It's crucial to keep an eye out for when they could reach the support level since the lack of obvious bottoms may signal a breakthrough rather than a trend reversal.

Let's now examine divergence.

When there is divergence, a gap is created between the moving average and the price action trendline. For instance, you have a positive price action trendline and a negative moving average. This shows that the price movement is slowing down. As a result, it serves as a cautionary tale to stay away from the gap's broader spots. In fact, you may want to consider selling your investments since prices might soon start to level out. This would be a blatant sign that it's time to list the property. Just watch out for any abrupt drawdowns if the price movement is approaching your take-profit level.

Divergence Trading using Bollinger Bands

With the Bollinger Bands trading method, you can forecast how the market movement will move inside a band or range. This indicates that the price rises to a resistance level, falls to a support level, and then resumes its upward movement. This kind of trading is a wonderful approach to generate consistent income since it is quite predictable. Although it may not be the most attractive approach to get money, this strategy works.

The moving average is your most effective tool when employing Bollinger Bands. The moving average trendline may be followed in order to identify the resistance and support levels with clarity. Consequently, divergence enables you to identify the precise moments at which you should enter and leave.

In other words, Bollinger Bands establish resistance and support levels based on repeated strikes to those levels. However, to properly use this approach, you must recognize at least three strikes on the support and resistance levels, on each side of any breakout or breakthrough signals.

To properly recognize this pattern, you need to utilize a longer term, like 48 hours. The price action trendline will move up or down depending on the trend of the moving average, even though this pattern is rather frequent, particularly among linked pairings. Therefore, your objective is to pinpoint the precise moment at when the trend will reverse. When that happens, you close the trade, take your winnings, and then watch for a decline in the price movement that brings it back up to the resistance level.

Bollinger Bands, as previously said, are not the most thrilling method to make money, but they can enable you to generate dependable profits that you can rely on to aid in the achievement of your financial objectives.

Mental State Levels
Despite all the data and analytics in the world, psychological considerations often influence investment behavior. These variables might be anything from

fundamentals like economic stability to completely irrational variables like expectations.

As a result, psychological levels are often linked to degrees of opposition and support. Investors could, for instance, establish a round number as a specific threshold that must be attained before they can purchase or sell.

Think about this scenario:

The Bollinger Band of a currency pair has been trading predictably. Price swings between a high of 1.48 and a low of 1.41. Because there are so little incentives to make any significant adjustments, investors may not feel pressured to take action. This is because investors consider the 1.50 point to be a barrier. They will sell if the price rises over this threshold. A wave of sell orders would then follow, bringing the price back down. In contrast, if the price drops below the 1.40 level, investors will start liquidating their holdings.

It should be highlighted that this psychological expectation could not have any technical justification. Investors, however, have seen the round numbers 1.40 and 1.50 as turning points that will determine how they ultimately respond. Because of this, technical analysis ought to grow to be your new best buddy. Without it, all you have are arbitrary judgments that can lack any genuine basis. You may not end up choosing the greatest investments as a consequence. On the other hand, if your psychological perception is grounded on technical information, you have a very high chance of making wise financial choices and forming judgments based on factual information.

Managing Risk in Divergence Trading

The biggest enemy of an investor is risk. Simply simply, the riskier the investment, the higher the likelihood of financial loss. For this reason, risk management is crucial to effective trading. In general, focusing on the facts will help you manage risk. More data analysis will make it simpler for you to identify patterns by merely glancing at charts. These charts often provide all the information you want. You won't even need to seek assistance from a professional. You will be able to navigate using information, experience, and instinct in combination.

Having said that, here are some sound advice on handling risk.

- To start, try to limit the amount you invest in one transaction. Even if the trade setting seems ideal, it's important to refrain from investing a lot of money in a single transaction. The more money you invest in a single transaction, the higher the amount of risk becomes. Therefore, remembering the 1% to 2% guideline will save you from making a horrible error. This is particularly crucial when you initially begin.

• Secondly, refrain from closing agreements based on erroneous indications. Before making a deal, always be on the lookout for all the indicators. Don't join the transaction if a signal is lacking or if you are uncertain. It's better to realize you lost a chance than to wish you had entered. There will always be a different chance.

• Third, choose the low risk option. It's preferable to err on the side of caution whenever possible. If you think the setting is ideal, investing 2% of your investment money will be sufficient to confirm your findings.

• Finally, it's important to diversify your portfolio. The majority of successful investors maintain many open positions across numerous currency pairings. As a result, you can manage risk more skillfully since you are not reliant on the movement of a single currency. Spreading risk across several currencies significantly lowers the possibility of losing out. So do your best to fill many places in different pairings. In this manner, the gains from one trade might be used to balance the losses from another.

Development Of Cryptocurrencies

What does it mean and how did it start?

Cryptographic methods are used to create each individual unit of currency in cryptocurrencies, as we previously saw in the previous chapter, and to transmit and verify those units of money between holders.

It's crucial to grasp the fundamental terms used in cryptography before learning more about cryptocurrencies. You may go on to the next part if you are already acquainted with these ideas (although a brief review of the basics wouldn't hurt). However, if you're not, it's advised that you read the next part at your own time. In the context of cryptocurrency, it discusses the fundamental principles of cryptography.

For the next chapter to advance, this is required.

a Synopsis of Cryptography

Simply said, cryptography is a method of dealing with codes and secrets that are intended to hide the underlying data (such as communications) for security purposes. Thus, anything from Morse code to cutting-edge computer techniques is included in the category of cryptography.

A communication is encrypted when it is turned into a code that only authorized parties may decipher.

Decryption is the process of transforming an encrypted code into its corresponding message. It is the exact opposite of encryption.

Cipher and Key: A cipher is an algorithm—a set of instructions—that may encrypt or decode data. It makes use of an additional component called the key, which feeds into the algorithm to produce one-of-a-kind encryptions. Without the cipher's key, it is impossible to decipher the code that was produced.

These mathematical procedures, known as hash functions, transform data of arbitrary amount into a fixed-length output. They are widely used in many computer science disciplines.

A cryptographic hash function is a unique kind of hash function that can be recognized by three characteristics:
(i) It is fairly simple to determine the function's output given an input.
(ii) It is quite difficult to determine a function's input given an output. It is

indeed thought to be computationally impossible.

(iii) It is exceedingly unlikely that two comparable inputs would result in the same outcome for the function.

Secure Hash Algorithm, or SHA, is a cryptographic hash function that includes a number of encryption operations. It was created by the N.S.A. With SHA256, input data is transformed into a "hash" output value that may be shared freely without fear of the input being discovered. The appeal of SHA is that its output can be easily verified, but its input is difficult to determine. As a result, it functions as a one-way lock. A well-known hash function is SHA-256, which produces outputs with a 256-bit size. Almost all internet security frameworks make use of it.

Public & Private Key: This is a method of communication that enables two parties to communicate (send & receive messages) without outside interference or disruption. The procedure comprises two parties that desire to communicate securely with one another (let's assume Alice and Bob). Each party is in possession of a set of cryptographic keys, one of which is public and the other secret. Everyone is aware of each other's public keys, but no one is aware of each other's secret keys. When a message is encrypted using Alice's private key, it can only be decrypted using Alice's public key, and vice versa, thanks to the way the arithmetic underlying this pair of keys works.

The idea is that Alice will use both her private key and Bob's public key to encrypt any messages she wishes to transmit to Bob in confidence. When Bob gets the encrypted communication, he will need both his private key and Alice's public key to decode it.

When interacting via an unsecured channel, having a mechanism to confirm the participants' identities is helpful. To achieve it, a digital signature is helpful. They are often inferred by ciphers or incorporated as certificates. For instance, Alice's private key may act as a form of digital signature since using it to encrypt a message would indicate to the recipient (who decrypts it using Alice's public key) that it is Alice on the other end and not someone else.

With this knowledge, we can go on to discussing cryptocurrencies and how/why they function. Those complex terminology may have overwhelmed you, but don't worry too much. If you have any questions in the future, you may return and consult this area. But let's start with how everything began in order to gain a clearer understanding.

Where Cryptocurrency Came From

We have used a variety of trade mediums throughout history, including fiat currencies, commodity money, paper money, and the gold standard. But with time, many societies (particularly scientific) from all over the globe have become disgruntled with these outdated currencies. It became conceivable to create a completely decentralized currency that may do away with the need for a central bank or government due to the growth of the internet and advancements achieved in the areas of cryptography, online security, and digital payments.

America became quite tight on the digital front after the 9/11 attacks. In order to conduct widespread web monitoring, laws like the Patriot Act were established. Naturally, because of their decentralized nature and perception as havens for terrorists and other unlawful activists, bitcoins were avoided.

The firm DigiCash was established in the Netherlands by American cryptographer David Chaum since it was most likely to be shut down in the United States. This was the first indication of cryptocurrencies. Blinding algorithms were utilized by DigiCash to safeguard user funds and transaction information. However, they interacted directly with the users and had total control over the currency's supply. The Central Bank of the Netherlands ruled against this, forcing DigiCash to either sell the business or shut it down quickly. Chaum believed that the $180 million offer Microsoft made to DigiCash was insufficient. As a result, Microsoft withdrawn the offer, and DigiCash finally ran out of money.

Many cryptocurrency systems, such b-money and BitGold, emerged shortly after but never really caught on. They possessed all the required elements—blockchain systems, privacy protection, decentralization, etc.—but for some reason, they weren't able to attract enough market interest to be widely adopted.

The first successful and extensively used contemporary cryptocurrency is called Bitcoin. In October 2008, a white paper outlining the specifics of how Bitcoin works was initially released under the alias Satoshi Nakamoto. The document is available for free at WWW.BITCOIN.ORG/BITCOIN.PDF and is titled "Bitcoin: A Peer-to-Peer Electronic Cash System." Satoshi made the first iteration of the bitcoin software available to the public in January 2009 on SourceForge.net. The identity of Satoshi Nakomoto's genuine self is still unknown. Satoshi is said to control around 1 million bitcoins, which are today valued at 2.8 billion dollars, according to bitcoin transaction records!

All significant businesses and startups are gradually embracing cryptocurrencies, particularly in Silicon Valley. In 2012, WordPress became the first significant business to take bitcoin. Big names like Microsoft, Dell, Virgin Group, and Lamborghini quickly followed. The entire market value of all cryptocurrencies has surpassed $100 billion at this time. This shows that, for a variety of reasons, the world is gradually moving toward decentralized cryptocurrencies.

Various cryptocurrency varieties

More than 900 cryptocurrencies are available to the general public, and hundreds more are generated each month. We shall examine the most well-known cryptocurrencies in this part. Visit WWW.COINMARKETCAP.COM to get the most recent market capitalizations and trends for the top 100 cryptocurrencies.

1. Bitcoin (BTC): This is the first cryptocurrency that is known to have gained widespread public acceptance and usage. It is regarded as the de facto standard and opened the door for contemporary cryptocurrencies. Nearly every other cryptocurrency has either

split off from bitcoin or has a lot of similarities with it. With a market worth of over 46 billion dollars, bitcoin is now the most widely traded digital money. Currently, one bitcoin is worth $2493 at this moment.

2. Litecoin (LTC): Litecoin is a decentralized peer-to-peer cryptocurrency that was introduced around two years after bitcoin. It has a growing community of developers, users, and advocates. It provides substantially quicker transaction confirmations than bitcoin, while being quite comparable to bitcoin. Litecoin has a market value of around $1.5 billion as of May 2017. Litecoin is the silver to bitcoin's gold. At the time of writing, one litecoin is worth $31.

3. Ethereum (ETH): Introduced very recently (in 2015), ethereum is similarly

a decentralized cryptocurrency but provides greater features, such as distributed computing, smart contracts, and the Ethereum virtual machine. The second-largest cryptocurrency at the moment by market value is ethereum, which is now worth 24 billion dollars. A single ether unit is currently worth $362 at the time of writing.

4. Ripple (XRP): Banks often utilize Ripple to securely and affordably settle international transactions. Its structure and protocol are distinct from those of bitcoin. In contrast to bitcoin, ripple doesn't need a lot of computational power to create new money. It has less network latency as a consequence. The Ripple currency's discrete units are known as ripples (XRP). With a market capitalization of 11 billion dollars and a unit price of $0.26, ripple is the third-largest cryptocurrency by market cap.

5. Dash (DASH): Formerly known as DarkCoin, Dash is a more covert version of the decentralized peer-to-peer cryptocurrency Bitcoin. It was introduced in January 2014 and rapidly saw an increase in traffic and fan support. Instant transactions (InstantSend) and fully private transactions (PrivateSend) are two of its most well-known features. In contrast to bitcoin's SHA256, it also employs a unique chained hashing algorithm dubbed X11. Dash has a market worth of almost $1 billion, and one coin costs $165 at the time of this writing.

Nota: Alternative cryptocurrencies introduced after Bitcoin are referred to as "Altcoins" and are referred to as such.

Bitcoin

By now, you must be aware that bitcoin is the most promising and popular cryptocurrency. So let's examine just what makes bitcoin such a fantastic currency and why investing in bitcoin is a no-brainer. Check read my book "Bitcoin: The Digital Gold" on amazon for a detailed look at bitcoin and how you may possibly earn thousands of dollars mining and trading bitcoins.

The advantages of Bitcoin as a currency

1. Limited Supply: There will only ever be 21 million bitcoins. In later chapters, we'll learn why. This limit on the total supply of bitcoins assures that their net worth will never fall below a certain level. The value of bitcoin rises along with the economy. In fewer than 20 years, it is predicted that one bitcoin will be worth around $1 million. And as of the time of this writing, it is less than

$3000. (Read Chapter 5 if you want to buy and invest in bitcoins.)

2. Durability: The main goal of currency is to represent money in a tangible or virtual form so that value exchanges may be carried out more easily. It might be a burden to continually produce new cash to repair damage caused by the currency fading or wearing out over time. All tangible currencies are vulnerable to physical harm from things like weather and wear and tear. Because it is entirely digital, bitcoin is superior to all other currencies in this situation. A bitcoin may possibly last an endless amount of time. It will continue to exist as long as the bitcoin protocol's operational network does. Bitcoin is one of the most resilient currencies ever made because to its decentralized network, high degree of encryption, digitalized money, and the

existence guarantee of the internet in the near future.

3. Interchangeable: As we already know, money is really a collection of monetary units. A currency that has interchangeable units is therefore a good currency. This implies that each unit should have a consistent structure and quantity of value. A good example is gold. Anywhere, 1 gram of gold is worth the same. In a similar vein, one bitcoin is identical to the other. In real actuality, there is no value difference between exchanging one bitcoin for another.

4. Divisibility: A good currency must be divided into units of the lowest needed scale (for example, dollars and cents, pounds and sterlings, or rupees and paisas) in order to be measured and graded for value. One bitcoin may be split into several smaller units called

Satoshis via the bitcoin protocol, and these Satoshis can then be further divided as needed.

5. Transferrability: You can transfer bitcoins with only a few clicks if you have a computer, an active internet connection, and a compatible device (a smartphone or tablet will also work). In contrast to bank checks and wire transfers, this makes it a particularly practical method of money transmission. It is also a more lucrative method of money transmission since there is no central authority or outside entity that levies a transfer fee.

What Is Cryptocurrency?

Cryptocurrency is a kind of digital money that functions without a central bank by using encryption methods to control the creation of units of the currency and confirm the movement of payments. They are decentralized and provide individuals a platform for wealth that is unconstrained and free from corruption.

According to the definition, a cryptocurrency is a kind of digital money intended to serve as a means of trade. Cryptography is used to establish the transactions and to make it easier to create new digital currencies. Compared to the familiar traditional paper money, it provides greater advantages. Does it sound magical to you? Impossible? Let me give you an example to help you understand the whole idea.

We're sitting on a park bench, you and I. It's a wonderful day. You get the orange I have in my possession and I now have none. I had one orange with me. That was easy, didn't it? Let's examine what happened in detail: You received my orange directly from my hand. I was there, and you were there, therefore you know it occurred. You became involved. To assist us with the transfer, we didn't need a third party to be there. Uncle Josh could have sat with us on the bench and verified that the orange got from me to you without us having to call him over. The orange is yours, and I'm sorry, but I don't have any more to offer you. I've lost all control over it. Simply said, the orange is no longer entirely in my hands, and you now have total authority over it. If you wish, you may give it to your buddy, who can then give it to his friend. so on.

So that's how an in-person conversation seems. I suppose it really doesn't matter if I give you a banana, a book, a cent, or a dollar bill—it's all the same. I have one digital orange, say. I'll hand you my digital orange right here. How do you know that digital orange, which was once exclusively mine, is now yours? Consider that for a moment. It's more difficult, am I right? How do you know that I didn't initially email that orange as an attachment to Uncle Josh? Or to Joe, your friend? Or to Lisa as well, my friend?

Perhaps I duplicated that digital orange on my PC a few times. Maybe a million people downloaded it after I posted it online. As you can see, there are several issues with this digital transaction. The appearance of delivering digital oranges differs from sending actual oranges. The double-spending dilemma is the term given to this issue by some clever computer scientists. But don't stress about it. All you need to know is that they've been perplexed by it for a while, and they've finally figured it out. However, let's attempt to come up with a fix on our own.

Finance Resolution

Maybe a ledger has to be kept track of these digital oranges. It simply functions as an accounting book where you keep track of all transactions. Since this ledger is digital, it needs to have a separate existence and a manager. The developers of the online game, Blizzard, have a "digital ledger" of every one of the precious blazing fire swords that are now in their possession. It's fantastic that someone like them could manage our digital oranges. Will that not lead to the solution?

However, there is a little issue: What if one man produced more on his own? Anytime he wanted, he could just add a few digital oranges to his account! Another issue is that things aren't precisely the same as they were the day we were sitting on the bench. You and I were the only two there. For all of our park bench transactions, using that computer is like removing Uncle Josh, a third party, from court. How can I just give you my digital orange the way I always do?

Is it possible to virtually recreate our bench in the park, just you and me, transaction? It doesn't seem like it will be that simple.

So how do you address this issue? How about if we distributed this ledger to everyone? The ledger will reside on everyone's PCs as opposed to just one. It will have a record of every transaction that has ever taken place in the history of digital oranges. It cannot be cheated. I'm not able to give you digital oranges that I don't have since then the system wouldn't be in sync with everyone else's. It would be difficult to overcome, particularly if it grew to be very large. Additionally, I know that no one can just decide to give themselves more digital oranges since it is not controlled by a single individual. The system's regulations were established from the outset. Additionally, the codes and regulations are open-source, much like the Wikipedia website or the Android operating system. The astute can contribute to, safeguard, enhance, and monitor it since it is there. You may take part in this network as well, update the ledger, and make sure everything is in order. You could get something like 25 virtual oranges in exchange for your efforts. Actually, there is no other method to add additional digital oranges to the system.

Let's take a closer look at the method I described, but first, a little breakdown. The cryptocurrency protocol is what it is called. The cryptocurrency that make up the system are those digital oranges. Fancy!

So, did you witness what occurred? What precisely can be done with a public ledger?

Remember that it is an open source? The public ledger's first entry specified the total amount of oranges. I am aware of its precise quantity. I am aware that they are constrained (rare) inside the system.

Now that I know that Digital Orange has officially left my hands and transferred to you, I may swap it with confidence. I couldn't say that about digital stuff before. The public ledger will be updated and used to confirm it.

I didn't need Uncle Josh (a third party) to make sure I didn't cheat, produce additional copies for myself, or send the same oranges twice or three times since it was a public ledger.

The trading of a digital apple is now equivalent to the exchange of a real apple inside the system. Now it's just as satisfying as really witnessing an orange fall from my palm into your pocket.

Additionally, the conversation only included two persons, exactly like on the park seat. There was no need that a third party be present; it was just you and myself.

It acts like a tangible item, in other words.

You know what's great, though? We can now deal with 1,000 oranges, 1 million oranges, or even 0.0000001 oranges since it is still digital. Even if I were in Nigeria and you were in New York City, I could press a button to transmit it and still put it into your digital pocket.

These digital oranges may even be made to ride on top of other digital objects! In the end, it's digital. Perhaps I can add some words on it, like a digital message. Or maybe I might include something more significant, like a contract, stock certificate, or identification card. So, this is wonderful! How ought these "digital oranges" to be valued or handled? They really are rather helpful, don't they?

Well, a lot of people are now debating it. Between this economic school and another economic school, a politician and programmers are arguing. But don't listen to everyone. Smart people exist. Some people are in the wrong. Some claim the system is worth a lot, while others claim it is worth nothing at all. A man really wrote a precise price: $2000 per orange. Some claim it's digital gold, while others assert it's money. Some people compare them to tulips. Some claim it will revolutionize the world, while others claim it is simply a fad. But they could have their own views on the matter. However, I believe you now know more about cryptocurrencies than the majority of them.

Therefore, when we discuss cryptocurrencies, we are referring to exclusively digital currencies. It is created using cryptography, which is the study and analysis of secret coding and coding methods. The history of cryptocurrency is very interesting because it was and continues to be a rebellion against the existing monetary system, which many people view as corrupt but necessary.

What led to the creation of cryptocurrency?

Since the Internet truly took off in the late 1990s and individuals began making purchases and bill payments online, it is natural to think that digital money has been present since that time. So it may come as a surprise to find that the idea of cryptocurrencies wasn't even brought up until 2008. The concepts and features of what would later be created and launched as Bitcoin were described at that time by Satoshi Nakamoto. At the time, software engineer and inventor Satoshi Nakamoto produced a paper for a peer-to-peer payment system named Bitcoin. However, he remained unknown. Bitcoin: A Peer-to-Peer Electronic Cash System was the title of the essay. In the abstract of the article, it is said that bitcoin is "purely a peer-to-peer form of electronic currency" and that it would "enable online payments to be transmitted directly from one party to another party without going through a banking institution. Digital signatures contribute to the solution, however the major advantages are lost if duplicate spending is still prevented by a third party. "We propose a solution to the double spending problem using a peer-to-peer network," he concluded. By hashing transactions into a continuous chain of hash-based proof-of-work, the network timestamps transactions, creating a record that cannot be modified without repeating the proof-of-work. The longest chain serves as evidence for both the order in which the events were seen and that it originated from the greatest CPU resource. They will produce the longest chain and outperform attackers as long as nodes in the network that are not working together to attack the network control the bulk of CPU power. There isn't much structure needed for the network itself. Nodes may leave and rejoin the network at any time, taking the longest proof-of-work chain as evidence of what occurred while they were away. Messages are broadcast using best efforts.

Despite being the first official cryptocurrency created, Bitcoin was essentially the lone fish in the pond for approximately two years. It seems sense that when individuals hear others discuss cryptocurrencies or digital currencies, the majority of people simply think of Bitcoin. Since they were the first, they received extensive media coverage. Of course, there are now more participants in the game; since 2011, digital currencies like Litecoin, Peercoin, Novacoin, and Namecoin, to mention a few, have established themselves. Approximately 900 distinct types of cryptocurrencies exist now, and that number is certain to increase.

Although it doesn't really matter whether or not the true identity of its founder is verified, cryptocurrency offers the promise of a cost-effective transaction as opposed to the frivolous fees charged to customers for both online and offline deals, as well as its decentralized nature. Although no one is certain of his identity, it is unimportant and only significant for historical records.

A bitcoin address is what?

The bitcoin address is helpful in locating and proving your ownership of a property, much as a real address is. Every client's experience is different. It is a public address for receiving cryptocurrency that contains a variety of distinctive characteristics. It establishes your ownership since each of these public addresses has a corresponding, matching private address that is likewise connected to the blockchain, which serves as a digital record. It functions similarly to a special mailbox where you get currency instead of emails.

A benefit of decentralization

The fact that the general public is already becoming irritated and losing trust in both the established paper-money system and the way centralized banks are handling people's lives and hard-earned money is no longer breaking news. Bitcoin is the first decentralized digital money in the world; it cannot be printed on plastic, paper, or metal and has no connection to any one person, group, or nation.

The existing centralized financial systems include choke points where the governments may exert pressure because of the existence of intermediaries. Consider how the issue of double spending is handled. They provide an intermediary the responsibility of maintaining a physical ledger of balances, and they take money from the payer's account and give it to the payee as part of each transaction. This kind of solution has a number of issues, including lengthy processes, third-party stalls, and extra transaction costs.

But because of the decentralized structure, there is no need for a middleman to resolve the issue of double spending. Every transaction always has a single payer and payee, making it literally digital currency. This is accomplished using a peer-to-peer network's publicly published ledger of transactions. Simply said, all transactions are recorded in a digital ledger to prevent the same individual from using the same digital money again. Due to the distributed nature of this digital ledger across all nodes, no one central authority is in charge of holding all the cash. In contrast to the now-common need for monitoring into the operations of Federal Reserve accounts, there is also openness. All linked parties have access to the public records of cryptocurrency transactions.

No third party, no government, no bank, and no organization may claim that it is in charge of overseeing the ledger or the regulation of cryptocurrencies. This means that once you send money in crypto currency to someone or to your wallet (we'll go into more depth about this later), it cannot be touched and is immune to the same financial circumstances that impact your banks. Any organization cannot track it since it is actually off of their radar. You are the only owner of it, and no one else. People all around the globe who saw the economic meltdown of 2008 and may have lost money as a consequence have started investing in and trading cryptocurrencies as a result of the decentralized nature of cryptocurrencies.

Additionally, there are instances of the government interfering with currency. Here are some illustrations.

In 2017, the Federal Government of Nigeria seized hard currency belonging to people, including Naira, Dollars, Pounds, and Euros. This was done in the name of battling corruption.

Border patrols seized the riches of Syrian migrants in 2016.

Venezuela had 720 percent inflation in 2016, which caused the bolivar to lose approximately 90% of its value.

Up to 40% of the money owned by Cyprus's citizens was taken by the government in 2013.

Argentina seized private pensions worth $30 billion in 2008.

True, governments are not the sole source of financial loss; severe risks such as hyperinflation and money seizures also exist. However, businesses or individuals may also steal money. The moment has come to offer people greater power over their money, and cryptocurrencies provide exactly that. Allowing individuals to manage their money has the following benefits:

It speeds up innovation. It is possible that more individuals would attempt to create new things if creating a new service or product will make them wealthy. Additionally, as more individuals try out innovation, competition will increase, which, as we all know, brings out the best in people. Since they have the assurance that no one can tamper with their riches, the market will be filled with high-quality goods.

People put in more effort when they are certain that their income is secure because they know that by doing so, they can enhance their own and their family' lives. However, when people's money may be stolen from them at any time and without their consent, it saps both their will to work hard and their motivation to do so.

When a certain area is seen as a certain path to success, people will strive to invest in it. This draws the best and the brightest. The greatest investors and the smartest enterprises will naturally gravitate toward a region where individuals are recognized to be in control of their money.

Therefore, bitcoin can essentially address every issue that the current financial system is facing. It assures transparency, does away with the need for a third party, saves time, is immune to confiscation, is less prone to hyperinflation, and provides universal access to all users. The ability to manage one's money is a basic human right that applies to digital currency.

Blockchain technology

It has been said that the internet is to email what the blockchain network is to cryptocurrency. The technology that underpins bitcoin transactions and streamlines our transactions is the blockchain network, to put it simply. It is an open, sequential ledger that is either numerical or digital (online) that keeps track of cryptocurrency transactions. It differs from the way banking is now done, in which every transaction is connected to a centralized, invisible network. But the digital ledger is stored in a decentralized database using blockchain technology, and it is accessible to everyone. Consequently, it enables detailed monitoring of every transaction. It is distributed in that you may manage every transaction transparently from the comfort of your own home. Each transaction is thought of as a single block, to which other blocks or transactions are added to create the digital, chronological chain known as blockchain. A new block is automatically produced each time a block is finished. A node is a computer that is a part of this network. As a result, each node that joins the network receives a copy of the blockchain whenever a new transaction is recorded. Anyone connected to the internet may reproduce and harmonize this decentralized database of the digital ledger, making it unnecessary to employ a centralized administrator (like banks). This digital ledger tracks not just financial transactions but also everything of value (assets) and is incorruptible (no centralized information is accessible for manipulation or hacking).

As a result, any node or computer linked to this decentralized network is guaranteed to have access to all information on each transaction, from its inception to its most recent completion. All other kinds of exchange need a third party or middleman to function. Simple duties like maintaining records and certifying transaction procedures are carried out by middlemen. However, using a blockchain network eliminates the need for a middleman in corporate transactions. The stocks, real estate, and money are shown on the computer as files. Therefore, it is much simpler to recreate these files, and there is no need for a middleman in the process at all.

It makes it possible for individuals to have mutual trust, which widens the scope of the transaction. It is also secure since it is impossible to compromise the system. For instance, if someone wishes to hack into a single transaction or block, he will attempt to change not just that block but also the one before it, and the one before that, all the way back to the transaction's inception. The bad news is that after that, he'll likely attempt to access any of the millions of machines that are linked to that network. In contrast to the centralized systems we do have now, the likelihood of someone breaking into the system is thus far lower. There have been instances of identity theft, bank record clearing, and hacking of financial systems. With the use of blockchain technology, none of these are feasible.

It will significantly influence the future generation. It provides equitable access to everyone on the network, in contrast to how banks and governments now operate. The removal of middlemen enables transactions to be carried out more frequently and efficiently, which contributes to the anticipated high traffic in both local and international trading. Additionally, it will increase freedom, since many nations invest millions of dollars in the battle against corruption. But with the blockchain network, defense against corruption and abuse is ensured. Even the vast majority of individuals who are not acquainted with the global economy will suddenly be better knowledgeable about the payment and banking systems. Blockchain is without a doubt the foundation for all cryptocurrencies. Ethereum creator Vitali Buterin said the following about blockchain: "A blockchain is a magic computer that anyone can upload programs to and let the programs run on their own. The current and all previous states of every program are always visible, and it carries a very strong cryptographically and economically secure guarantee that programs running on the chain will continue to execute in exactly the way that the blockchain protocol specifies. Check out "Blockchain: The Complete Guide To Understanding Blockchain Technology" for a more in-depth look at the technology:

Cryptocurrency And Blockchain

Cryptocurrency

Cryptocurrencies are money units without a central lender, such as a nation's central bank. They are produced using computer-encryption methods that restrict the quantity of money units (or coins) produced and then confirm any transfer of the money after their production.

Due of its conceptual resemblance to the mine of gold or other valuable metals, this creation method is referred to as "mining". Cryptocurrency mining requires figuring out ever-more difficult algorithms or puzzles. It takes a lot of processing power for computers to solve these algorithms. In other words, we can't simply produce value out of thin air since it requires money to mine them. Therefore, rather than a central bank or government, the value of these currencies is guaranteed by the principles of mathematics.

There are more applications in the real world as cryptocurrencies become more widely used. You can buy anything with bitcoin, including actual things, gift cards, tickets to sporting events, and even hotel reservations. It is now also a form of payment accepted in certain pubs and restaurants. Now, several NGOs now accept Bitcoin and other cryptocurrencies as forms of payment. Additionally, there are increasing unlawful usage due to instances of covert internet markets selling illegal items, including Silk Road and AlphaBay.

Compared to the currencies we are familiar with and use today, these currencies offer a vast variety of benefits. They are so appealing to both long-term investors and short-term speculators because of this. Cryptocurrencies do, of course, have certain disadvantages, just like any investment, which we shall discuss later in this book.

What it Does

Contrary to what many people think, Bitcoin was not the first cryptocurrency. Twelve years before Satoshi Nakamoto published the Bitcoin white paper, e-gold was first offered in 1996. Over a million people used E-gold at its peak, which was backed by real gold holdings. Because it was anonymous and the financial system had not yet been updated for the digital age, thieves could use it to commit crimes like identity theft and money laundering with ease. E-gold was also centralized, which made it a popular target for hackers. It was shut down forcefully by the US government.

There are now several types of cryptocurrencies, some of which you may have already used. To unlock certain Facebook games and applications or to upgrade Farmville, users may buy Facebook credits. Microsoft Rewards is a program that gives users virtual points in exchange for utilizing certain services. These are in fact digital currency!

But Bitcoin changed the game because it made blockchain, a new technology, available. In reality, the Bitcoin protocol was developed precisely with blockchain in mind. Because a blockchain is a decentralized piece of software, unlike e-gold, it is not administered by a single organization. Instead, hundreds of node computers spread out its functioning globally. Decentralization brings a lot of advantages. One is that there is no central server to hack into, making hacking almost impossible. A hacker would need to have 51% of the blockchain's nodes under their control. Another advantage is that without again controlling 51% of the Blockchain's nodes, the data it contains cannot be altered or falsified. As a result, the data kept on a blockchain cannot be changed. It is unchangeable. A process known as a fork may be used to create new protocols, but data saved on the blockchain is kept there indefinitely.

The fact that double spending was an issue was the key to Bitcoin's success. Double spending, which allows for fraudulent transactions, is the practice of using the same token more than once. Nakamoto's verification method employs a concept known as proof of work to stop duplicate spending.

New cryptocurrency tokens can only be generated when people use them, as opposed to new dollars, which are created either by the government increasing or decreasing interest rates or by printing new money (which really causes inflation). The only cryptocurrency that will ever exist was produced when the program initially debuted, and certain cryptocurrencies, like the XRP, are coded such that no new ones can ever be created. However, the majority produce fresh tokens by mining.

Since mining is really how bitcoin transactions are confirmed, supply growth continues to keep pace with demand. Because the value is not controlled by the government like that of the dollar, it is really much more natural. Undoubtedly, cryptocurrencies are money, and they may even be more real and genuine than conventional dollars.

Blockchain

The blockchain is a growing list of transactions that is updated daily. The transactions that were carried out on cryptocurrency exchanges like Ethereum or Bitcoin are associated with the blocks on the blockchain. Every block is related to the block before it thanks to a hash reference that is included in every block. Each transaction will include a time stamp so that users can determine when the trade was accepted into the chain.

The earliest safe blockchain research was conducted in the early 1990s by Stuart Haber and W. Scott Stornetta. In order to determine if there was a more effective technique to get data from a single block, both students were using Merkle trees.

While working on the fundamental building blocks of Bitcoin's public ledger in 2008, someone connected to the Satoshi Nakamoto group imagined the first blockchain distribution. Once a time stamp has been applied to a transaction, the blockchain is connected to a peer-to-peer network that will be disseminated through a server.

Blockchain's database is independently run. Therefore, if you use the blockchain for cryptocurrencies like Bitcoin, you can be sure that no double spending will take place until you or a system administrator approves it.

The term "blockchain" was first used to describe a cryptocurrency platform in a document that was released in 2008 by a member of the Nakamoto group. The blockchain for Bitcoin has a 20 GB file in 2014. The record now stands at more than 100 GB.

The new program that would run on the distributed Blockchain's database was referred to as "Blockchain 2.0." It was explained as a language that you would be able to develop in order for users to create complex smart contracts. Following the creation of the smart contract, an invoice would be generated in order to send payment whenever the crucial conditions of the agreement were met. Blockchain 2.0 technology moved beyond simple transactions to create exchanges that would ultimately serve as a kind of arbitrator for both data and money.

When blockchain was developed, it was anticipated that by turning on a privacy protection that would allow people to monetize their information while giving them the ability to ensure that the creators were compensated for their intellectual property, people could be excluded from the global economy.

The second generation of blockchain enabled the storage of a user's digital identity and persona as well as a path toward addressing the issue of social inequality. In order for an off-chain oracle to be able to access data and events that are not on the network and forecast market conditions for blockchain to interact with the market appropriately, a new protocol was built in 2016.

The Russian Federation said that they will be putting a project using Blockchain's platform for electronic voting into action. Blockchain is also being used by the music business to monitor copyrights and distribute royalties.

Orphan blocks are those on the blockchain that were not chosen to be included to the chain. Peers will continue to support the blocks' many iterations throughout time. Since they will be rewritten in the database before being resubmitted to their peers for improvement, only the version with the highest score will be maintained. Although there is no assurance that the block's entry will be preserved, this will prevent the blocks from overwriting one another and cause redundant data to be added to the blockchain.

Workings of Blockchain

The blockchain will remove the dangers of storing your information in one location whenever it is kept on a network. Due to the decentralized nature of the blockchain, ad hoc messages will be used on the distributed network.

The network of a blockchain will not have the weak spots that hackers may target in a centralized system. Public key cryptography is one way that will be used to secure blockchains. Each user is identified by their public key, which is a random string of letters and numbers. A person who wishes to transfer you coins will get the public key.

Anything connected to that address will be recorded in the value tokens that are distributed across a blockchain network. Users will be able to access assets that other people cannot access by using their private keys, which will be password-protected. Because if someone else gets your private key, they will have half of what they need to access your digital money and other assets, you will need to keep it to yourself.

Your phone's password and phone number are another analogy for private and public keys. The public key is your phone number since it will be known by others, but the private key is your phone's password, which makes it impossible for anybody to access it.

Data manipulation happens in centralized systems since they are governed by a single entity. But once a system becomes decentralized, it will reach the point where everyone connected to the network can access the data that is there, negating the possibility of keeping anything secret from the users.

A copy of the blockchain will be stored on each node in the blockchain system. The database and a computational trust will keep the data's quality up to par. Since there won't be a centralized copy of the data, no user will be more trustworthy than any other. The network will broadcast transactions for everyone to see. Before a broadcast is sent out from that block to the nodes so that the operation can be confirmed and then a block can be produced from another node, mining nodes will work at verifying transactions and constructing blocks using the messages that are sent out on a best effort basis. Blockchain will use timestamping techniques so that system modifications may be serialized. Proof of stake and evidence of burn are two further blockchain-based methods.

The blockchain will continue to expand, and as a result, there will be a danger of node centralization due to the increased cost of the computer resources needed to run larger data files.

Starting With Bitcoin

A person using the alias "Satoshi Nakamoto" established the peer-to-peer cryptocurrency system known as Bitcoin. The paper describing the system's guiding principles was released in late 2008 and is currently available on the network. The code for the open-source program Bitcoin Core, which now serves as the foundation of the Bitcoin network and allows for transactions, was subsequently built by Nakamoto.

This brief comment from Nakamoto sums up one of his motives for creating the Bitcoin system: "Bitcoin is very attractive to the libertarian viewpoint if we can explain it properly."

The use of Bitcoin enables transactions to be carried out securely from one party to another, and both the management of transactions and the issuance of money are carried out by means of a P2P protocol thanks to peer-to-peer technology that operates without any central authority and intermediaries such as banks or governmental institutions.

What exactly is a bitcoin?

A bitcoin, or simply BTC, is the money used in the Bitcoin system. It is a digitally generated string of alphanumeric characters that symbolizes a prior transaction and is entered into a public record. The latter, known as Block Chain, uses an address—a form of pseudonym—to record the owners of the money throughout a transaction without disclosing their identities. Each bitcoin is a series of transactions, or more accurately, a series of digital signatures: each bitcoin symbolizes the transfer of a specified number of bitcoins from one owner to another using a digital signature system that validates the transaction's legitimacy. The future owner's public key and the value of a certain function called the "Hash function," which was added into the previous transaction, are what are signed.

Using a decentralised peer-to-peer network that timestamps transactions and produces a computational evidence of their chronological sequence, Nakamoto also proposes a solution to the double-spending issue in the article. The bitcoins are not governed by any entity. Anyone who installs the program on their computer has access to manage them. Even criminal users may access the network thanks to the system's design, but they won't be taken into account until the majority of users are trustworthy.

Although they wouldn't be able to directly take bitcoin from other people's wallets, if tomorrow a group of individuals or businesses managed to amass the majority of the computer power in the Bitcoin network, they would be able to reverse their transactions and block future transactions.

During the debate, we suggest a more technical study of the Bitcoin creation and administration system as well as the cryptographic technologies that made the emergence of this decentralized electronic money possible.

Here is the operating system:

- Each node, or participant in the network, retains a copy of each financial transaction.

Every time a block is confirmed and added to the chain, it is communicated to all nodes that add it to the stored copy. A node is a computer/chip connected to the bitcoin network via software that stores and distributes an up-to-date, real-time copy of the blockchain.

The fundamental characteristics of bitcoin are:

- There can never be more than 21 million bitcoins in circulation.

- Valid transactions cannot be restricted or censored by anybody.

> The source code for Bitcoin should always be available to everyone.

- No one is able to block participation in the network.

- Anyone may join the Bitcoin network without providing any identity.

• Each component may be used with another.

• Transactions that have been confirmed cannot be altered or removed. History cannot be erased.

Bitcoin's past and present as they relate to the blockchain

You can only begin with the Bitcoin protocol if you want to comprehend the possibilities and potential of Blockchain technology. One of the greatest connections exists between these two realms.

And there is no other way it could be. The first cryptocurrency to be developed and used for commerce is Bitcoin, which operates via Blockchain technology. Blockchain and Distributed Ledger technologies owe their success to this digital money. Therefore, the Blockchain's fictitious history is also Bitcoin's. We shall attempt to retrace it in this essay, however it will be everything but a straight path.

Bitcoin and blockchain: a six-stage history of the first cryptocurrency

However, a crucial question must be answered before discussing Bitcoin's history: What are Bitcoins, exactly?

1. From concept to reality: Bitcoin

Bitcoin was created at the end of 2008 when Satoshi Nakamoto, a person or group of persons whose identities are still unknown, issued a white paper outlining his concept for an algorithm-based, peer-to-peer encrypted virtual money. The notion put out is essentially a declaration of war against the banking industry, which at the moment was being overtaken by a severe crisis. The Bitcoin network starts operating in 2009, the community expands, and a pizza is the first tangible commodity to be purchased using bitcoin. Bitcoin hits a $1 billion valuation in 2012.

2. Early interactions with the media and authorities

But the first issues appear. Initially (2010–2011), Bitcoin was consigned to a fringe phenomena of little interest to the commercial world due to its association with the criminal market, from narcotics to terrorism, as a result of its use of pseudonyms and lack of a regulatory body.

Regulators in many countries are already beginning to ponder how Bitcoin should be viewed, with some classifying it as a financial instrument, some classifying it as a currency, and yet others banning it or warning banks against using it.

3. Blockchain and Bitcoin

The Blockchain, the technology that underpins Bitcoin, is the subject of a phase that began in 2014. Platforms that make use of some of Bitcoin's fundamental ideas start to emerge: Ripple, a platform developed in 2012 to permit interbank transfers in several currencies, has gained support from the first institutions. Ethereum, a platform focused on the construction of smart contracts.

The R3 consortium, made up of the top banks in the world, was also established in 2015 to work on the Corda platform. Additionally in 2015, the Linux Foundation begins work on the Hyperledger project to build a platform collaboratively that businesses may utilize. Thus, we reach a fork in the road where some believe just in cryptocurrencies and others think the underlying technology may be used in other contexts.

4. The blockchain fad spreads

The Blockchain craze becomes popular in 2016. It begins to get media attention, and more often than not, it is presented in a way that clearly distinguishes it from Bitcoin (at the end of 2015, The Economist devoted the cover to it and listed it among the innovations that would alter the digital world in the next years). As a result of this media buzz, businesses start to become more aware of Blockchain, and several tests begin.

5. Between swings and complexities: blockchain and cryptocurrencies

The so-called disillusionment phase of Gartner's hype cycle begins towards the end of 2017. The first questions about the transformative potential of this technology that fails to deliver on its promises start to surface. As their value fluctuates over time, cryptocurrencies are being used as a tool for financial speculation. As the network expands, the so-called mining process, which is used to validate transactions on the Bitcoin network, encounters significant limitations (slow transaction processing, high energy consumption, and potential for centralization of machines used for this purpose).

"Crypto-winter" 6.

After receiving significant media attention in 2017 because to the increase in their price, 2018 is defined by an irreversible capitalization crash. The Blockchain community created the phrase "crypto winter" to describe this period. Winter hasn't yet come to the cryptocurrency technology, however. Companies are still very interested in the Blockchain. The developer communities that swirl around the open Blockchain are also helping to advance technology. In the meanwhile, the future is yet to be written.

The rise of bitcoin and its benefits

First, it is important to evaluate the several factors that have contributed to part of bitcoin's success.

• Usefulness: Due to its anonymity-preserving features and lack of a physical transfer requirement, bitcoin may be used to purchase or sell products and services, even illicit ones (together with traditional currencies like dollars and euros). The Silk Road website, for instance, exclusively accepts bitcoin.

• Exchange: Through a variety of websites, you may exchange bitcoins for other currencies and vice versa.

• Speculation: As a result of bitcoin's rising value and rising popularity, speculators are purchasing the digital currency in the aim of subsequently selling it for a profit (while actually running the danger of suffering significant losses).

• Scarcity: There is a finite amount of bitcoins available. The maximum on production is around 21 million, and it is algorithmically regulated.

The fact that Bitcoin is a decentralized currency and based on cryptographic evidence in the world of cryptocurrencies means it does not suffer from the flaw present in a model based on trust in guarantor authorities as far as the system's most advantageous features are concerned. As a result, compared to other online payment providers, transaction costs are significantly reduced. Any quantity of money may be sent as well, and it does so rather swiftly and securely. Transactions are conducted using an address, which allows the owner to remain anonymous. The money is unchangeable and unfalsifiable: because each transaction is immediately recorded on the Blockchain, which is open to the world and available to everyone, it cannot be undone once it has been sent. Government interference and competition from other cryptocurrencies are the two biggest dangers to the growth of Bitcoin.

Bitcoin is well recognized for being a network that makes legal operations like online gambling, money laundering, and drug sales possible.

Government authorities may decide to forbid Bitcoin use if it becomes a hard money and is used more often as a substitute for the dollar. Additionally, since the network first adopted Bitcoin, a number of other currencies—all of which are controlled by central banks—have been developed and widely adopted owing to the internet; if any of them achieved more notoriety, Bitcoin would swiftly lose its dominance.

Overall, its key benefits include

One of its key benefits is that there is no central bank in charge of the currency, as we have often said. Since no one can regulate its value, the currency's buying power is constant. In reality, it makes more sense for it to increase in value over time as its supply is restricted to 21 million bitcoins.

• They cannot be faked: Although this is technically possible, it is extremely difficult to remain undetected in a network run by millions of users; sooner or later, you would be found.

• There are no geographical restrictions on the use of bitcoin for payment; everything that can be done using bitcoin as a method of payment is possible.

• No middlemen are required: We may make the payment directly without the need of any intermediaries, such as banks or credit card companies. making transactions a lot less expensive.

- Security: Compared to the cryptographic systems employed by banks, the currency's technology is significantly more secure.

- Open source: Anyone with access to the network may see transactions, make changes, and perform other operations. always by means of a consensual process.

- Characteristics of a virtual currency: Being a virtual currency, its mobility and longevity are far higher than those of actual money.

The following are the primary drawbacks as of now.

- Despite the fact that some businesses are now taking bitcoin payments, the technology is still not widely used.

- Because there is no regulator to support it, people are less trusting of the money.

Given its qualities, it has been used as a method of payment on the black market of cyber-attacks and has been connected to weapons smuggling, child pornography, terrorism, and drug trafficking. It has had tremendous volatility since its debut.

The three sites where Bitcoin is used operate

How is Bitcoin operated? Let's attempt to envision a hypothetical "register" where relationships between "addresses" and values (or the number of tokens) are recorded. Each address corresponds to a certain value (i.e. a specific quantity of tokens) at any particular moment. A portion or the whole of the value may only be transferred to another address by someone who is aware of the (non-public) key that is exclusively linked to each (public) address.

Therefore, Bitcoin has made a number of advancements that will serve as the foundation for the creation of new Blockchain platforms. the first three.

1. Synonyms

Anyone may freely create an address without the permission of another institution (as is the case with IBAN and banks), which is the first basic aspect of how Bitcoin works.

Decentralization 2.
Decentralization is the second key innovation, and it is made feasible by the process of agreement on the modifications to be made to the register, dispersed among a variable number of potentially selfish players, or those actors that are only interested in themselves. Since the system lacks a centralized authority, it specifically addresses the issue of confusion over which version of the register is the correct one among multiple potential ones that may emerge.

3. Computer programming

The third distinguishing characteristic of Bitcoin is its programmability. For instance, the owner of a Bitcoin can send money to another address, arrange for more bizarre transfers, such as awarding money to the first person to solve a particular computational puzzle, or to the majority of addresses in a group, or block it for a set period of time. Bitcoin Script, a scripting language whose definition is a part of Bitcoin, may be used to explain these mechanics.

Between Bitcoin and Ethereum

We go from the revolutionary notes to the sad ones. Even while Bitcoin has numerous advantages, its restricted expressive capabilities (which are on purpose since a language's limitations make its execution's results more predictable) limit the potential for automation.

The Ethereum project, which has practically all the technological capabilities of Bitcoin but adds a significant innovation: a scripting language termed "complete Turing," is able to express any logic accessible with any other computer language, was created out of the need to overcome these constraints.

The implementation of distributed, uncensored applications, or so-called dApps, as well as the ability to write arbitrary programs whose execution is guaranteed by the network and which can receive and transfer funds are all made possible by this system. This system also makes it possible to automate various types of mechanics, primarily financial and insurance ones.

How to get around the drawbacks of early cryptocurrencies using Bitcoin and its offspring

Certainly many intriguing qualities are offered by the way Bitcoin works in combination with Ethereum's innovations, but there are also certain restrictions. more specifically

Proof of Work uses a lot of energy; only 10 transactions per second are handled; and privacy is not sufficiently safeguarded.

Numerous alternative "galaxies" have developed in order to solve these issues and get around the limits of the original Blockchain systems.

1. Cut Back on Proof of Work

Two ameliorative strategies are investigated to lower the energy cost of Proof of Work: either construct a problem-based version of it whose answer has advantageous side effects, or substitute another mechanism.

Primecoin, which suggests using computing effort to solve prime number search issues, is one of the initial method's most important initiatives. The primary drawback of the second strategy is its reliance on the so-called Proof of Stake method, which the Peercoin network pioneered and which entails currency holders guaranteeing transactions with a stake.

2. Increase transactional throughput

Proof of Stake may decrease the time it takes to record transactions, which not only lowers the energy cost of consensus but also increases the frequency (throughput) of transactions.

Platforms like Iota and Nano, which aim to lower transaction costs, as well as Stellar and Ripple, which use different consensus processes from those based on both Proof of Work and Proof of Stake, have developed in an effort to enhance throughput.

3. Privacy protection Platforms like Monero and Zcash utilize sophisticated

cryptographic algorithms to conceal critical information and guarantee the integrity of transactions in order to address the privacy problem and prevent trades from being monitored.

Basics Of Cryptocurrency

By the end of 2017, Bitcoin was making headlines all around the globe over the Christmas season. The media has discussed it due of its price's rollercoaster. Although you may have heard about the fuzz, you may not be aware of the details. With regard to digital currencies, there is a lot to understand. To properly grasp the essence of the situation, you must master many ins and outs. Not to mention the technical language associated with cryptocurrency. Take heart! You are not alone yourself. In reality, only approximately 50% of people can explain the fundamentals of cryptocurrencies and blockchain technology well, and only about 10% engage with them on a daily basis. That indicates that many individuals still don't fully get how cryptocurrencies work.

Here is a quick summary of the explanation. Using a cryptocurrency is similar to using PayPal, with the exception that the transaction is fully anonymous and the cryptocurrency you are using isn't based on a conventional currency. For a further explanation, the word "cryptocurrency" refers to any kind of digital currency that is built around cryptographic techniques and computer code and that bases its pricing only on what can be justified by supply and demand. Without blockchain technology (explained below), cryptocurrencies would not be conceivable. Speculative investors tend to exercise a larger than average amount of influence over the price movement of cryptocurrencies since there is now a lot more interest in investing in them than there is in utilizing them for conventional reasons. This is enough to make the market as a whole quite volatile.

With a market capitalization of more than $30 billion, or more than half the total for all cryptocurrencies, Bitcoin has remained at the top of the heap because it served as the initial proof of concept for the technology. As of January 2018, it is worth about $14,500, making it the most expensive cryptocurrency available. The Ethereum Platform is the main rival to Bitcoin, and it is currently gaining popularity among businesses and consumers thanks to its dedication to blockchain technology in general and to smart contracts, which are straightforward programs that can be activated when specific external events occur.

Of course, these are just the two biggest; there are already more than a thousand distinct kinds of cryptocurrencies available on the market. While some of them are only little Bitcoin clones hoping to profit from the next big thing, others have their own distinct advantages that enable them to stand on their own two feet and provide the ideal service to a certain niche of users.

Unlike cryptocurrencies, which often experience movement depending on events that occur across the globe, conventional currencies, sometimes known as fiat currencies, are always going to be constrained in their movement owing to their explicit links to the economy of a certain nation. Anything may impact a cryptocurrency's price as long as enough of its investors think it is important. Cryptocurrencies range in value from being worth less than $0.01 up to Bitcoin's maximum value of $20,000 per unit for these and other reasons.

Generally speaking, there are two types of cryptocurrencies: centralized and decentralized. All of the cryptocurrencies available on the market right now are decentralized, which means they run entirely independently of any kind of controlling entity. As an alternative to this, there are centralized cryptocurrencies like the one China is now developing or the CryptoRubble that Russia revealed it was developing at the end of 2017. Decentralized systems nearly always call for extra degrees of verification to ensure that any transactions that are processed are accurate and not being used maliciously.

Blockchain information

The technology behind cryptocurrencies is called blockchain. A decentralized database known as a blockchain may have nodes almost everywhere in the globe. Despite the fact that the technology is just a few years old, it is already being considered for implementation at almost every level of society, from financial services to healthcare. Its capacity to provide anybody who needs it read-only access to crucial information while guaranteeing that the data itself stays exceedingly safe has earned it a reputation for security and accessibility.

Each blockchain block comprises a broad range of distinct transactions as well as data that enables the blockchain to accurately order its blocks automatically. This convoluted procedure begins with two people carrying out a bitcoin transaction. When a node has gathered enough transactions, they are uploaded into a block, which is then verified by a third party, also referred to as a cryptocurrency miner, who uses a powerful computer to ensure that the block is legitimate before adding it to the blockchain.

If, and only if, 51% of all presently active nodes agree with the data in this block, it is then subjected to a second round of review and added to the blockchain. The data is then uploaded to the blockchain and updated in each node's storage to reflect the new blockchain if this is the case. This occurs hundreds of times per day each time a new block is added to a blockchain.

These features of blockchain technology make it very beneficial for the kinds of tasks that call for self-sorting functionality while also enabling the blockchain to work without any outside interference. Instead, as the nodes communicate with one another, the blockchain organizes and validates its own data, enabling any number of people to connect with it without being concerned that things won't be able to work themselves out.

While other transactions will just show quantities with no information at all given out to make it feasible to trace a certain transaction to a single individual, interested users may see but not touch when it comes to the full specifics of their own transactions. Then, those who operate a node for the relevant blockchain may add new blocks to the chain, but only if a majority of the existing blocks concur that the new data makes sense.

Blockchain technology is incredibly safe by nature, but this is only because technology as a whole hasn't advanced to the point where this kind of attack is feasible. A situation where enough bogus nodes were active to demonstrate that the correct version of the blockchain was really wrong would be required to produce a false block. Even while the expense of such a venture today surpasses the benefit, it is doubtful that this will always be the case.

Every blockchain has a second procedure in place in addition to the 51 percent rule to ensure that no block can be modified once it has been added to the chain. This is because a hash function is used to encrypt each new block that is added to the blockchain. This has various implications, beginning with the fact that without the proper decryption key—which is only known to the blockchain's creator—nobody would be able to read the whole blockchain, even if they managed to get it.

The SHA256 hash is the most used hash function, and it helps the blockchain arrange blocks correctly as well as acting as a digital fingerprint for the data it carries, meaning that if the contents changes, so does the hash. The blockchain's overall hash is then updated to reflect the change once each new block is added to the chain and given its own unique hash. A tool known as a Merkle tree can then verify this hash, enabling it to swiftly compare the hash on file to the current hash and instantly identify any unauthorized modifications that could have been performed in the meantime. The system is then cleaned of modified data and a confirmed copy is put in its place. In essence, this implies that information entered into the blockchain will be there indefinitely.

Pricing

It is crucial to bear in mind that, although not being regulated in the conventional sense, the prices of different cryptocurrencies nevertheless follow the laws of supply and demand when following their values. In fact, many experts think they better embody these concepts than their native currencies since they aren't subject to the same manipulation that more conventional currencies do. But just because no one is in charge doesn't imply that external factors aren't influencing the price of cryptocurrencies. In reality, since there is no way of knowing what can trigger them, they are often much more directly related to global events.

Furthermore, cryptocurrencies will be far more susceptible than other forms of assets to be impacted by this kind of speculative manipulation when it comes to price generally. This is brought on by the fact that considerably more individuals invest for speculative goals than they do for useful goals. This leads to a pricing bubble that pushes the price beyond what supply and demand would otherwise allow. Smaller cryptocurrencies face a somewhat worse version of this issue since there may only be a few thousand users worldwide, making every new purchase potentially significant.

The fundamentals of trading cryptocurrencies are quite similar to those of trading in general. others intending to acquire cryptocurrencies attempt to purchase them from existing holders at a discount from others trying to sell their units at the highest price the market will bear. The amount that might be won or lost in a single day can be enormous if prudence isn't used throughout the task since cryptocurrencies, particularly the smaller varieties, are known to witness price movements of up to 15% every day.

It is quite difficult to find a cryptocurrency listed on the main exchanges that isn't going through some kind of price bubble in 2018, given how heavily the cryptocurrency industry is geared toward speculators. However, as long as the price you invest at is near enough to the market value price that you won't be caught with your pants down should the bubble collapse and the price return to normal, this is not always a negative thing. If you get in too late, you run the danger of losing money since the price will plummet well below what you paid with little sign of a turnaround anytime near.

A broad range of external variables may also have an impact on price, either favorably or unfavorably. The employment of automated trading bots to increase liquidity is one of the most frequent ways this impacts the majority of cryptocurrencies. Liquidity is essential for a cryptocurrency to thrive, but it needs a careful balance since a liquidity level that is too high shows that nobody is interested in investing in the cryptocurrency, while a liquidity level that is too low shows that nobody can purchase, even if they want to.

Automated trading bots, which are most often used in China, provide several solutions to this issue. First, they engage in back-and-forth trading, creating liquidity that other traders may observe and use as a foundation for their own assumptions. Actual traders who are attempting to close out one or both sides of the equation may also take advantage of these deals. As a result of the benefits from mining the block, the bot trading process actually contributes to the creation of more cryptocurrency units since the bot transactions still need to be verified by miners just like any other blockchain transaction.

Although artificial deflation in the bitcoin market may be countered through liquidity and other external factors, it can also be leveraged for nefarious ends to carry out a pump and dump scheme. With this approach, an investor purchases as much of the target asset as they can before exerting all of their effort to drive the price to absurdly high levels, which they may then capitalize on by selling all of their assets at once.

This tactic is particularly effective with cryptocurrencies because there are no connections between any two exchanges, making it all that is required to successfully carry out a pump and dump to purchase all of the coins currently in circulation on a single exchange before carrying out the pump and dump as intended.

Using Ethereum to Mine Ether, Chapter 6

If you don't want to, you are not required to purchase ether. It is always possible to mine it; here is how.

On your PC, install C++ visual.

Either a 32-bit or a 64-bit machine will be used by you. When you download C++ to mine properly, you must also get the required Microsoft visual. You should utilize a 64-bit computer whenever feasible since the 32-bit system has various drawbacks while you are mining ether. However, if that is all you have, you will need to be patient while the application sorts out its problems.

Set up Ethereum

Downloading Mist will be the next action. Your wallet for ethereum will be located in Mist, your graphical user interface. You should download Mist, a user-friendly browser extension that provides support, so that you may locate other individuals who can assist you if you ever need it.

acquire blockchain

You'll need to download the blockchain onto your computer in this phase, which will take some time to finish. Ten gigabytes worth of data will be downloaded by you. Therefore, it is a good idea to find something else to do if you start downloading this record while it completes its necessary tasks.

Get your wallet ready.

You have to prepare your wallet right now. There are several alternatives available to you when deciding which wallet to use. To choose which wallet will be best for you to use, you must consider both the security that wallet offers and the advantages that wallet will provide. It is essential to have a wallet since that is where all of your ether will go when you are paid for your task.

Install AMD, CL SDK, or Nvidia

Before installing the software that will use the GPU, you must inspect your GPU. Your choice of program will depend on how powerful your GPU is.

Activate AlethOne Miner

You should get AletheOne since it's probable that you work alone. The technology you are developing to enable mining is called AletheOne. A 32-bit system should be avoided for mining since it will freeze and cause additional problems.

Await the startup of the DAG.

You will need to wait for around 10 minutes once AletheOne is finished before you can create a DAG. The DAG file will be kept in the computer's RAM so that an ASIC-resistant algorithm may be built.

Rejoin a mining pool

Finding a mining pool that will work for you is important since it's likely that you won't be working in a warehouse filled with GPU. This relates to the contest that you already read about. You don't want to join a pool that won't survive until you have to contend with too many miners. This will be the case because you will be placing yourself in a situation where you may not be rewarded for the job that you do or, if you are, the reward will not be as large as it might be if there are other individuals who are more talented than you.

Chapter 3: Trading Cryptocurrencies

You must first register on a cryptocurrency exchange that works in your nation in order to trade in cryptocurrencies. There are several exchanges available to US citizens, including some well-known ones like Coinbase, Gemini, and Bitfinex. However, since Bitfinex is situated in Hong Kong and has recently had several attacks, it would be safer to trade on another exchange. However, as all exchanges deal with a lot of money and are eventually online, they are theoretically all vulnerable to various hacks and attacks. Hackers steal millions and billions of dollars by finding only one security flaw that will let them in. The market capitalization of cryptocurrencies is now about $500 billion, which is excessive and has drawn a lot of attention on a worldwide scale. If you put your money in cryptocurrencies, you run the danger of being subject to the DAO assault, but nothing in the world is secure or safe in such case. Even a well-known corporation like Lehman Brothers might declare bankruptcy tomorrow.

The most secure way to protect your cryptocurrencies is to use an offline or hard wallet. One excellent example of an offline wallet that allows users to store all cryptocurrencies is Ledger. You may transfer all of your money from online wallets to your offline hard wallet by following some easy procedures, and it can be connected to your computer like a pen drive or hard disk. If you don't intend to sell or use your coins anytime soon, you may keep them safe using this approach.

However, before you can begin trading, you must first sign up with a local exchange that enables you to purchase or sell cryptocurrencies. Zebpay and Koinex are two well-known brands in

India. You may also trade cryptocurrencies on Binance and Bitfinex, and other exchanges like Bittrex provide you the ability to purchase or sell hundreds of different cryptocurrencies. Select a currency exchange that offers support for many currencies and cheap transaction costs. As of December 2017, one such exchange that has reasonable fees in comparison to other exchanges is Bittrex.

After registering with your phone number and email address, you will need to verify your KYC. To do this, you may need to upload a copy of your government-issued identification card or verification card as well as the bank account information you will use to transfer funds to your exchange account. Once your KYC has been registered and validated, which typically takes one to three days, you are ready to start trading cryptocurrencies. Some exchanges have significant pricing discrepancies, such as Indian exchanges that never use global prices. There is usually a price differential of 100,000 rupees (about $1,500), and sometimes the purchasing and selling prices also diverge, preventing consumers from exchanging "in a day."

Only when the selling and purchasing prices are the same is intraday trading feasible. The user may submit a purchase or sell bid at the going rate. Users are only able to do it on a select few exchanges. Some exchanges allow users to day trade and make a lot of money by having the same pricing to buy and sell.

Every cryptocurrency's price changes daily, rising and falling. Although there may not be a clear pattern, if you are patient enough, you may watch the market movement for a few days and

then try your luck with a little amount of money. You may gradually raise your investment while keeping some money away and trading with others.
Personally, I would suggest not "selling" all of your coins when trading; instead, preserve a portion of them to increase in value in accordance with the coin's natural trend, since you may not be able to repurchase them at the same price. When the price rises, you will thereafter get a much less number of coins for the same amount of money than you did previously. This occurred to me when I was trading Bitcoin; I sold some of my coins in the hopes of buying more at a cheaper price, but the price never decreased and instead rose so high that I had to put in twice as much money to acquire the same number of coins again! The second piece of advice is to never pay market value when you can bid. Don't bid too low, however, since the

price may not drop that much. Bid around $100 to $200 less on Bitcoin and a few dollars less on other currencies that are under the $1000 threshold because, although $200 less on Bitcoin may not have a significant impact on the currency as a whole, it will provide you "slightly" more coins than the market price. Again, it could seem like it doesn't matter, but consider the future, when one Bitcoin will be worth somewhere near a million dollars. A difference of even 0.005 Bitcoin will be noticeable then!

Beware of panic selling is the final piece of advice I'd like to provide at this time. The weak investors flee and panic sell once the price begins to decline because they fear that it will continue to decline and they will lose their investment. They are completely correct, as it has occurred in several instances, such as when Ethereum plummeted from $21 to

$8 during the DAO assault, and a similar event also occurred with Zcash, but prices won't rise over a certain point until there is a significant news event or significant collapse. As it grows, it encounters opposition, and once it overcomes it, it remains at that level. The current resistance level for Bitcoin is approximately $17,000. Unless there is major news, an assault, or a crash that directly affects Bitcoin in some way, it won't go below this level in any circumstance.

The Fibonacci sequence has a pattern that Bitcoin follows, which indicates that the next high will be twice as high as the previous low. The Beta factor rises every time it begins to move higher by following this pattern. Given that the price has climbed to $19,000 at this point, a $500 decline would represent only a 2.5% decrease, which is negligible. Although $500 can seem like a considerable amount and a significant drop, this drop is negligible when you realize that the price of Bitcoin is now $19,000.

When you consider that Ethereum is now trading at $700, even a $200 drop seems like a collapse! If it quickly declines from $700 to $500, it lost almost 30% of its worth. Therefore, the amount of lost cash depends on its current value.

A $500 loss for Ethereum is a collapse, whereas a $500 loss for Bitcoin is a dip. Similar to other currencies, there are highs and lows, and if you trade intraday, you may make a lot of money if you're careful. And if you don't want to trade but instead simply want to save the coins for the future, I would suggest getting a hard wallet or offline wallet so you can store the money safely without worrying that you'll lose it all in the event that the exchanges fall!

Why Do Cryptocurrencies Exist?

Many people now think that national currencies like the US dollar, the British pound sterling, the euro, the Canadian dollar, and more will soon be replaced by cryptocurrencies like Bitcoin. This is due to the emergence of cryptocurrencies as fiercely competitive alternatives to fiat money.

Obviously sponsored by governments and central banks, traditional currencies have problems that led to the development of cryptocurrencies. As a result, traditional currencies are susceptible to a number of issues, such as corruption and manipulation.

As opposed to traditional currencies, which are sponsored by governments, bitcoin and other cryptocurrencies are not controlled by any one person or entity.

Bitcoin is decentralized, transparent, and open source. In order to verify the authenticity of any particular transaction, you may see every transaction that has ever occurred on the network and look at the blockchain data for yourself.

Bitcoin employs very complex mathematical algorithms to regulate the creation of new bitcoins and guarantee that there is never any double spending on the network (recall that this was the fatal weakness of failed virtual currencies prior to Bitcoin).

If you think you can produce an endless supply of bitcoins, you're very mistaken. Since the Bitcoin code is so complex and safe, it is almost hard to trick the system.

One of the underlying problems with traditional currencies is that there is an infinite supply of them. This indicates that monetary policy decisions are made by governments and central banks.

When more money is created and released into the market, inflation results. As a result, our paper money loses some of its purchasing power and we are forced to pay more for goods that we previously just needed to spend a few dollars on.

Bitcoin, however, is a special instance. According to the Bitcoin Protocol, there can only ever be 21,000,000 bitcoins created, hence in practice, bitcoin is a finite resource.

Additionally, bitcoins may be split into smaller sums, much as pennies can be divided into dollars. The smallest bitcoin unit, known as a Satoshi, is one hundred millionth of a bitcoin. This suggests that until you have purchased a full bitcoin, you may make little deposits of a few thousand Satoshis.

Naturally, if you choose this strategy, it could take some time for you to achieve 1 BTC, but if the price continues increasing, consistently buying a few

Satoshis can end up being beneficial in the long term.

The great mobility of cryptocurrencies, which enables you to take them everywhere you go, is another aspect that adds to their attractiveness. You may use gold the same way you would use real money. However, a significant quantity could strain your pocketbook or bags.

Try toting a briefcase filled with a million dollars or a bag of gold! It is not at all as simple as it seems in movies.

With cryptocurrencies, you may easily send money whenever and wherever you want since there are several wallet alternatives that are quite portable.

Bitcoins are exempt from bank and governmental regulations. This implies that you won't be required to pay the substantial bank fees that you typically pay when transferring money to other people.

You don't need to wait several hours or even days for your payments to clear or publish since bitcoin transactions happen very instantly (often in 10 to 45 minutes).

www.ingramcontent.com/pod-product-compliance
Lightning Source LLC
Chambersburg PA
CBHW050245120526
44590CB00016B/2225